The Sidewalk Ends at GOD

Pretty Witty Christian Ditties

Garden replica of the Chartres Cathedral labyrinth.
Unlike a maze, a labyrinth has only one path.

~ ※ ~

By *Emmanuel DeWeg*

Copyright Emmanuel DeWeg 2025. Per Acts 4:32, this content may be used at any time, in any way, without compensation, for the glory of Jesus Christ.

A great thanks to the Berean Bible, who has granted all use of their bible verses at no cost: https://berean.Bible/licensing.htm

This book was designed to be photocopied on 8.5" x 11" paper, 2 book pages per side, 4 book pages per piece of paper, a total of 25 papers needed per book.

A free printable version of this book and videos read by the author are available at: EmmanuelDeWeg.org

To provide comments about this edition, to make contributions with unlimited free use, or to subscribe to release information, please go to the publisher's website: EmmanuelDeWeg.org

HB ISBN: 9781640324053
PB ISBN: 9781640324060
EBook ISBN: 9781640324077
This copy is Edition 1, Revision 0

Poems with an * are not by this author. All Greek and Hebrew (H) words are numbered with the Strong and Thayer system, so these words can be easily searched online.

TABLE OF CONTENTS

1. How Can It Be?.. 5
2. How Can Man!?... 6
3. Teen Oxen 7
4. I Decided 8
5. Blather Infection (and cranberries won't help)...................... 9
6. Right 10
7. I'm Amazed 11
8. Who U B 12
9. Whom 13
10. To Whom 14
11. New 16
12. Word Up 17
13. Avoid Dance 18
14. Cabin Feever 19
15. Atheist T-Shirts 20
16. Slick Trick 21
17. Voices I Listen 22
18. Pnuema Machine 24
19. Thanks 25
20. *Trinity 26
21. Runaway Mouth 27
22. Enough! 28
23. Navel Disease 29
24. Brownies 30
25. In Christ 31
26. I Am 32
27. Fight 33
28. Pay 34
29. A Million Seeds of Love 36
30. *Gospel 38
31. Prove It 39
32. Wanna Bet? 40
33. Stay Strong 42
34. Can 43
35. Same 44
36. *The Weaver or The Tapestry 45
37. Now 46
38. A Cubit Taller 47
39. Bounded Set 48
40. Money 49
41. Goads 50
42. More Atheist T-Shirts 51
43. Eyes On 52

44. SLOWLY 53
45. COME TO CHRIST 54
46. DESIRE 56
47. *KATRINA'S SUN-DIAL 57
48. ODE TO DUCKS 58
49. KNOW 60
50. IT IS FINISHED 61
51. VANITY 62
52. LOST 63
53. SPEED 64
54. AGE 65
55. GOD'S MAJORITY 66
56. CHANGE 68
57. SEE ALL 70
58. CAPTAIN 71
59. TODAY 72
60. LONG NOSE 73
61. SING 74
62. HEALED 75
63. PLANKS 76
64. MOVING DAY! 77
65. RELATING WHERE 78
66. HEART 79
67. LITTLE BIRDIE 80
68. BOBBLEHEAD 81
69. BRAINS IN CHAINS 82
70. DRINK OF GOD 83
71. ANXIOUS 84
72. REVOLUTION 85
73. REFUSE THE RUSE 86
74. ORANGE 87
75. RELATIONSHIP RECESSION 88
76. ODE TO LARD 89
77. RIGHT QUESTION 90
78. MAMMON 91
79. PSALM 150 92
80. ACCEPTANCE 93
81. MINUTES 94
82. AIM FOR NO REGRETS 95
83. YOUR TURN 96
84. FIGHT! 97
85. BEGIN THE END BEGIN 98
ABOUT THE AUTHOR 99

1. How Can It Be?

Behold, I have inscribed you on the palms of My hands.
—Isaiah 49:16

How can it be
God wants relationship with me?

Yet from the beginning, The Lamb
pierced <u>my</u> <u>name</u>
into the palm of His hand

To leave all and come down from above
for me
how can it be?
It can only be Love.

2. How Can Man!?

How can there be God
with Evil in the world?

You're right.
There isn't God.
Can't be.
So then,
Who is,
Doing all this evil?

Seems like
Man
does just fine
satisfying desires
at the expense of others.

Add God
then see
evil lessoned
He set us free!
How many near misses?
'Lucky breaks' out of the blue?
God's hand was guiding.
He really cares for you.

When in darkness
God lights up our 'should'.

God exists.
Loves us,
'swith us.
In God
stop evil
make good.

3. Teen Oxen

Where there are no oxen, the manger is empty, but an abundant harvest comes through the strength of the ox. —Proverbs 14:4

When there are no oxen
the trough is clean
Where there are no teens
the kitchen gleams

But much increase comes
when oxen abound
Riches *are* found
with teens around

Separation, contradictions, pressing boundaries
they are just breaking free
Teens reject parents
to safely define what is 'me'

The Parents at home
may not *feel* their blessings
Babies get out of diapers
teens end their transgressing

The Liar has tricked them
one too many times
Godly pursuits are learned
to be a feast, sublime

If you teach from youth
if you *model* the same
submit to the Spirit
and you'll win the game.

4. I Decided

Does might make right
or right make might?[1]

I don't want to sit in a circle
patting everyone on the back.

If a thing is true
let it be so:
'yes' be 'yes'
and 'no' be 'no'.

I decided God isn't there
because life is unfair.
He wasn't there when I needed Him
To stop people from being them.

So now I do what I want
'cause He can't see.
All is freedom, freed from Him
No accountability, I count, only me.

That makes it true, right?
If mighty self-affirmations are my norm?
Just don't let it get too quiet
I prefer to live in a storm

'cause I don't want to hear
Who's been whispering in my ear

---

[1] Abraham Lincoln, Cooper Institute Speech, New York, February 27, 1860

5. Blather Infection
(and cranberries won't help)

Lips flip flap
with only Blip Blap
Blither Blather
Froth & Lather
Nothing to say
but silence to slay

A joy to none
except the one
who fills the room
with their gloom

Where is the bit
to pull back this horse
Where is the rudder
to turn back this dudder
One little tongue
for darkness and sun

There's no way to win
answering fools that begin
Blither Blather
Froth & Lather
The words are a tell
to run and be well

Unless you found
it's your own sound!

6. Right

And we have come to know and believe the love that God has for us. God is love; whoever abides in love abides in God, and God in him.
—1 John 4:16

Good Poetry
elevates
alleviates
resonates

Bad Poetry
weird
impersonates
~!

Good God
love
dove
indwells

Bad God
cruel
demanding
snakes!

John Tells
real
wrong
how

This Day
choose
trust
live

7. I'm Amazed

How many people
claim to be
seekers of truth
don't ponder
what is fact
who is science
refuse to test
Jesus the Christ

Opinions of men
draped as god
protects against
submitting,
alleviates the pain
of yielding,
freedom to
do what you want
but is a mirage;
Darwin has
no martyrs.

Choose which
fairytale
cult leader
or truth
Jesus is one
or turn your back
Be enlightened
in your dark.

8. Who U B

A Dee H Dee
What's wrong with me
That you work so much
2 Try 2 Fix Me

Can't you understand
I was made from God's own hand
Could I be
Sum thing He In ten did?

My limbs are on the move
Mama, I'm in the groove
Sitting still just ain't
In turn rest sting

Why want to slow me down?
Taking pills of white or brown
Are these for my success or make me
4 U 2 Hand dull?

I took the meds you said
Now I'm active as the dead
Since when is comatose
Bet her Act shun

Some day I'll return the same
When you barely remember my name
Make you eat some meds
2 Not B My Burr done

A Dee H Dee
Creates victories
Combining
Holys peer right & Boy dee

9. Whom

Constantly we're bombarded
constantly we must decide
      from whom to listen
      to whom to follow
      for whom to act
the good or evil side.

10. To Whom

Do you not know that when you offer yourselves as obedient slaves, you are slaves to the one you obey, whether you are slaves to sin leading to death, or to obedience leading to righteousness?
—Romans 6:16

Who you gonna live for?
What you gonna do?
Makin up your own rules?
Or livin' in the truth?

You're not exploring
You're just making do
Getting by
Getting High
And living like a fool

Wake Up! Get Down!
And play by <u>His</u> rules
Give up!
Lay down!
The King made you His tool

Quit your dreaming and your scheming
It ain't gonna do
Lying, cheating, stealing
It's not for what He made you

Stand Up! Fight Back!
God will hold you up
Hang tight!
Live Right
You're gonna make it through

Who's your Master?
'Cause we're all slaves
Always serving somebody
But you gotta choice
On who you obey

Who you gonna live for?
What you gonna do?
Listen to which voices
Find which is true

Make up your mind
You're wasting time
So choose!

11. New

Behold, I am about to do something new; even now it is coming. Do you not see it? Indeed, I will make a way in the wilderness and streams in the desert —Isaiah 43:19

Doing something new
A <u>new</u> song in their hearts
Love without damnation
Which rules can not provide

Do you hear it?
O Lord sing to me
I want to dance in your Love
I want to Sing from my Soul
I want to Cry like a sponge, with love and joy, and pain
I want to live in your Love

Oh Lord sing to me your song
How do I get out of my mind
and live in yours?

12. Word Up

I'll do what I want
    God's got a word
Marry who I want
    God's got a word
Watch what I want
    God's got a word
Listen to what I want
    God's got a word
Dress how I want
    God's got a word
Join who I want
    God's got a word
Spend how I want
    God's got a word
Play how I want
    God's got a word
<u>Live</u> how I want
    God's got a word
And God's got the last word.

13. Avoid Dance

Throwin shade
on what God made
to keep you away
from having to obey

What about this?
What about that?
Claiming these are 'facts'
only trying to distract

Your fear is hiding behind chatter,
argument, noise, and clatter;
arrogance behind philosophical hypotho-sisses
and paradigm twisting mistaken missives

Blabbing from the roof
enjoying your own personal 'truth'
making a big show
but you don't *really* want to know

The Truth, is Love!
sent from above
A gift to accept
or choose to reject

God is still there
no matter what you 'declare'
Inviting you <u>to</u> Him
for you to live <u>through</u> Him

Pride resists what is real
I live it, so know how you feel
but it's time to take a stand
and bow you knee to God the Man

14. Cabin Feever

Everything is driving me crazy
even the way you stand, hurts me a ton
the weather outside is awful
and there's a dark cloud eclipsing the son.
It's cabin feever

I recognize the symptoms quickly
the way my limbs, hang listless to the floor
TV remote too far to reach at
pizza waiting, still waiting outside my door
It's cabin feever

My fever runs 98.7
but nothing matters, can life go on?
How do I shake this stupid stupor?
Dancing wildly to a gospel marathon!
Bye-bye cabin feever

15. Atheist T-Shirts

I'm MY refuge and my shield; I put my hope in ME. —Atheist Psalm 119:114

For all have sinned and fall short of the glory of ME. —Atheist Romans 3:23

I'm MY strength and MY song, and I have decided MY own salvation. —Atheist Psalm 118:14

Do not fear, for I'm with you; do not be afraid, for I'm MY god. —Atheist Isaiah 41:10

For I so loved the world that I gave NOTHING, so that everyone who believes in ME shall STILL DIE.
—Atheist John 3:16

16. Slick Trick

You know what's right
You know what's wrong
There's Always trouble
If you play along

You may look pretty
Nine times out of ten
There's still a consequence
Waiting in the end

Ride it fast
Get the high
Don't you wanna
Be one of the guys?

"I make good money"
"I get good grades"
"It don't affect *me*"
That's what they say

You know what's right
You know what's wrong
It's death you're serenading;
you keep singing his song

17. Voices I Listen

Those old voices that I hear
they whispers in my ear
says I'm no good
says, "you should . . ."

Well, they are leaving today
going away
after They pretended to be my friend
it was Jesus that <u>proved</u> who I am

'Cause God made me special
God made true
I need His grace and love
instead of judgements from you

Those old voices, they lie, ya' see
they're not from love, nor sympathy
but today
I send them away
pack their backs and get from here
No longer will I allow those old voices in my ear

Is that my mother's?
my father's? an old boyfriend?
it don't matter
God now defines me, instead of every one of them

God's taken over, but
He was always right here ♥
God's forgiveness
God's grace
God's love
I only had to choose
His love
whispering,
whispering in my ear.

'Cause God made me special
and God made true
I'm listening to His love now
to help me get through

18. Pnuema[2] Machine

Step right up and take a look,
you won't believe what you have seen.
The Amazing — The Stupendous —
Pnuema containing, am-bu-la-tory relationship machine!

A complexity of construction
yet precisely planned
developed by the wisest mind
it can move, it can sit, it can stand.

And should it get scratched,
its fluid start to leak,
internal medics find the puncture
fixing it as we speak.

Dump in some ruffage
it converts its own fuel
knowing what's the good stuff
and ejecting the stool.

So many systems
each a different design.
No random act, they interact.
Yes, systems *combined*. Sublime!

How could it be?
Phenomenal — Impossible — Fantastical — but True!
God wanted a special relationship,
that's why He created You.

---

[2] Spirit; πνεῦμα; pneuma: Strong's 4151. Pneuma is the noun form of 'to breathe' or 'blow' (pneó 4154), the life force or soul that God breathed into Adam and all humankind. Literally, ghost, wind, breath, and spirit.

19. Thanks

Liars will prohibit marriage and require abstinence from certain foods that God has created to be received with thanksgiving by those who believe and know the truth. —1 Timothy 4:3

The abstain-etarian accuses the glutton	Luke 7:34
The bibber mocks the dry	Luke 7:33
Why through food freedom	1 Cor 8:9
destroy love?	Rom 14:20
Carne or herbs, water or wine	Dan 1:16
no food wins you God's approval	1 Cor 8:8
but can poison your heart	Matt 15:11
Caution! in judging each other by food	Rom 14:3
or treating others as less	Rom 14:10
each says they know best	1 Cor 8:2
but we do not.	1 Cor 8:1
God does.	Rom 14:22
He prepared the fattened banquet	Matt 22:2
to be received with thanksgiving	1 Tim 4:4
Let us put *God* on top	Exod 20:3
Act in Love	Rom 14:15

20. *Trinity[3]

Three folds in my garment,
Yet only one garment I bear,
Three joints in a finger,
Yet only one finger is there,
Three leaves in a shamrock,
Yet only one shamrock I wear,
Frost, ice, and snow,
These are nothing but water.
Three persons in God,
Yet only one God is there.

---

[3] From the 1908 "Religious Songs of Connaught" by Douglas Hyde, Vol. 2, pg 397.

21. Runaway Mouth

*Set a guard, O LORD, over my mouth; keep watch
at the door of my lips. —Psalm 141:3*

Runaway mouth,
runaway mouth!
Running around
all over the house —
always telling others
what *their* life's about!

Just 'cause you think it
don't mean it needs to be said
Some things are better off
left in your head

The world doesn't revolve
on All about you
Others need love
So *listen* too!

Be quick to listen
and slow to speak
life will be better
and friends you will keep

Chase after those lips!
don't let them get away
sing this little ditty
to make them obey —

Runaway mouth,
runaway mouth!
Stop That running all over the house![4]

---

[4] Can you recite the whole poem in one breath?

22. Enough!

You're good enough and
I'm good enough since
there is One who made it so your . . .
life was designed with
His plan in mind as
God made us perfect but things get messy when . . .
we do our best but
still fail the test as
wants get in the way of niceness so . . .
God made a way to
make better this day
and get us all to heaven by . . .
joining with Him in
life to the brim as
His hand of earthly presence but . . .
pride keeps our knee from
bending to He which
would end your mental struggle proving that . . .
you're good enough and
she's good enough and
he's good enough and
they're good enough and
we're good enough all
in Christ!

23. Navel Disease

Vanity of vanities; all is vanity. —Ecclesiastes 1:2

I can listen to me for hours,
Milk injustice created on demand,
Spend all day staring at my navel,
Or spread faux illness over life so bland.

I don't bother hearing others,
It's cozier within my own views,
My whole world is so filled with me,
Why would I even bother, listening to YOU?

24. Brownies

If I had not come and spoken to them, they would not be guilty of sin. Now, however, they have no excuse for their sin. —John 15:22

Sin sin
where to begin
or more importantly
where does it end?

Take brownie batter
mix in turd from the ground
no one will eat them
regardless the nugget size found.

Life with God
no matter how sweet
is quickly soiled
choosing darkness to eat.

Put God's light in your life
as quick as you can:
apologize, be humble,
live in the Lamb.

His light in darkness
destroys all residual sin
where not-love began
it now has seen its end.

25. In Christ

I in Christ
and
Christ in me
Oh the peace
that there could be

with
I in Christ
and
Christ in me
God is part
of every thing

No more trying
No more denying
No more do-do-doing
No more lying
Submission
is the key

to
I in Christ
and
Christ in me
Bring me peace
and
set me free!

26. I Am

The
I
AM
is now
always present
as we need to be also
now, present, in this moment
with this person
connecting
real.
Am
I
?

27. Fight

Turn away from evil and do good; seek peace and pursue it.
—Psalm 34:14

You must Fight for peace
What thief robs you day and night?
How hard it is to find a clear path
You must fight
for less
to get more
Seak peace
pursue it.

28. Pay

Paga y paga
paga y paga, paga
Utility man
coming hat in hand
said what I owe
continues to grow
    sorry friend
    we're all the same
    just the way
It's time to pay.
Paga y paga
paga y paga, paga

The bills are due
just got through
paying t'other two
now there's more
coming through the door
    been here before
    just the way
It's time to pay.
Paga y paga
paga y paga, paga

Worked eight to 5
now kids need fed
then second job
roof over our head
    patches ripping
    socks on the fray
    ¿school dance tomorrow?
It's time to pay.
Paga y paga
paga y paga, paga

¿Is that the fair?
Let's go inside
a roller coaster?
I want to ride!
funnel cake?
ice-y-freeze?
getting hungry
no es gratis
     so . . .
Paga y paga
paga y paga, paga
paga y paga
paga y paga, paga

Gotta get out
of the squirrel cage spin
this working nights
needs to end
Don't want the stuff
Don't need the bling
    ¿You found a puppy?
    Just the way
There's more to pay.
Paga y paga
paga y paga, paga
paga y paga
paga

29. A Million Seeds of Love

Once God held my reign
leading me down life's road
then I got away from Him
yanking to and fro

I wanted to get 'there'
succeeding in all 'God's' plans
missionary, church planter
pulpit filling preacher man

I got the numbers
I delivered the goods
I filled the pews
just like I should

But all this 'I'
was not really about 'Him'
Exhausted is what it left me
shining my own light before men

Then God said
in no uncertain terms
"Get back in line
ain't my design
for you to be doing
these showy things.

"Go talk nice,
live pure in life,
and plant a million seeds of love
that the world don't count for nothin'
but is greatest to Me above!"

He was right of course
I'm just the horse
God is my worth
not glory from works
Now I love wherever I'm led
walking with God in His glory instead.

30. *Gospel[5]

So let our lips and lives express
The holy Gospel we profess;
So let our walks and virtues shine,
To prove the doctrine all divine.

Thus shall we best proclaim abroad
The honor of our Saviour God;
When the salvation reigns within,
And grace subdues the pow'r of sin.

Our flesh and sense must be denied;
Passion and envy, lust and pride;
While justice, temp'rance, truth and love
Our inward piety approve.

Religion bears our spirits up,
While we expect that blessed hope,
The bright appearance of the Lord,
And faith stands leaning on His Word.

That sacred stream, Thy holy Word,
That all our raging fear controls:
Sweet peace Thy promises afford,
And give new strength to fainting souls.

---

[5] Isaac Watts Hymn published in the year 1707. Often you'll only see the first two lines.

31. Prove It

God is love.
Love is God.

Prove love,
prove God.

Prove mercy, humor, kindness?
Prove good, bad, right?

Some refuse to <u>ask</u> the questions.
Others refuse to <u>allow</u> the questions.
For many, no proof is enough.

Do beliefs change God?
What'll take to change you?

Your heart proves your pride.
Your pride proves your heart.

Your life proves your god.

32. Wanna Bet?

He who walks with the wise will become wise, but the companion of fools will be destroyed. —Proverbs 13:20

I'll be you eternity
that you're _not_
as good as it gets.

Maybe you could use some help
now and then
to be nice
while in pain, hungry, or depressed?

You avoid obligation with excuses
that just make no sense at all:
"There are many roads up the mountain."
But who knows where they all go?
If we're "all touching the same elephant"
how do _I_ know
that _you_ know?

You say you're guided by a "later prophet"?
Been hearing "special messages"
(which oddly benefit _you_ really well)?
If they change based on donations
where's the guarantee of avoiding hell?

Sure, there are many ideas to follow
but it's ridiculous
to pick and choose
and then combine them all.
That's like playing cricket in scuba gear
using ping-pong paddles
to hit the bowling ball!

So many many opinions
can't all all all be true
The truth, the way, and the end
are actually all the same:
Simply Christ.
Christ inside of you.

Heaven or hell,
love or hate,
pride or humbleness,
even eternity is up for debate?

Wanna bet?

33. Stay Strong

Nevertheless, I have reserved seven thousand in Israel — all whose knees have not bowed to Baal and whose mouths have not kissed him.
—1 Kings 19:18

There are others that still fight
in the common ground of right.
They may not even be Christians
but all it takes to extinguish darkness
is the strength of one light.

Men should stay out of women's restrooms.
Bad people should go to jail.
Children need protecting.
Y chromosomes make you a male.

We <u>each</u> need to keep fighting
so stand strong and have faith
there are thousands like you
that make this world a better place.

34. Can

Can you be butt-ugly
and be loved by God?

Let me answer that.
Yes you can —
look at me!

35. Same

In the same way, good deeds are obvious, and even the ones that are inconspicuous cannot remain hidden —1 Timothy 5:25

Imagine a billboard
attached to your brain
that displayed every thought —
life wouldn't be the same!

The brain only gives soil
to the flesh and the heart.
Which seeds to plant?
Which must depart?

A crop that's juicy, dry, or rotten
must be fed in order to take root.
Cultivating desires and pursuits
will always bear their fruit.

To grow a lasting legacy
with no secrets and no shame
life in private and in public
should be harvests of the same.

36. *The Weaver or The Tapestry[6]

My Life is but a weaving
Between my Lord and me;
I cannot choose the colors
He worketh steadily.

Oft times He weaveth sorrow
And I, in foolish pride,
Forget He sees the upper,
And I the under side.

Not 'til the loom is silent
And the shuttles cease to fly,
Shall God unroll the canvas
And explain the reason why.

The dark threads are as needful
In the Weaver's skillful hand,
As the threads of gold and silver
In the pattern He has planned.

He knows, He loves, He cares,
Nothing this truth can dim.
He gives His very best to those
Who choose to walk with Him.

---

[6] By Grant Colfax Tullar (1903), quoted often by Corrie ten Boom

37. Now

... nor ... will inherit the kingdom of God. —1 Corinthians 6:10

Do thieves or drunkards or —
go to heaven?
Do priests?
Are these something you do?
Or are they something you be?

What are you?
Dust animated, hunger driven; do?
Soul free, heart yearning; be?

Who knows heaven?
God
leaves out what you do,
and asks what you be.

Then let us ask
God
about heaven.

"Lord,
you've promised me heaven
accepting your gift of Jesus Christ.
But life now
now
is empty
distracted from you.

"Is this blinding plank
from my own heart's yearnings?
Can my soul tune to your Spirit
and sample heaven now
now
where all that I *be*
becomes all that I *do*?"

38. A Cubit Taller

And who of you by worrying is able to add one cubit to his stature?
—Matthew 6:27

We get so worked up about flarp,
prisoners within walls of our own blarp,
stressing our way into a lather,
about things that don't really matter,
giving ourselves indigestion,
over the smallest things in question,
fretting and obsessing about every wrinkle and hair,
when God tells us
it's about *Him* we should care!

39. Bounded Set

And every house is built by someone, but God is the builder of everything. —Hebrews 3:4

Science . . .

May tell the what
but never the why

Says if you could
not if you should

Flaunts how little we know
about how big is God's show

Though science we applaud
the creator is GOD.

40. Money

*Dishonest wealth will dwindle, but what is earned
through hard work will be multiplied.* —Proverbs 13:11

Money, they say, makes the world go spin
and great works you can do with it, if not drawn to sin
so heed these lessons, build your wealth, and let compounding begin!

Some people squeeze money like sand
but it leaks out between the fingers of their two hands
from memberships, monthly fees, and subscription plans.

Others think big, and buy their oversized dream
but its appetite gobbled more money than it seemed
leaving them with 'experience' and a pocket empty of green.

Many desire just to 'think' and grow rich
but money without learning, toil, and earning comes with a glitch,
to 'think' and grow clothes, you must labor with care on every stich.

Look! Here's the secret how people have gotten most rich: Slow
by spending less than they earn, being careful on what it goes
then earning rates above inflation — simple — and now you know![7]

---

[7] U.S. inflation averaged 3.3% since 1924. Beat this year in and year out and you're earning 'real interest' over the decades, even though a single year's inflation ranged from -10.9% (1921) to 17.8% (1917).

41. Goads

We all fell to the ground, and I heard a voice say to me in Hebrew, 'Saul, Saul, why do you persecute Me? It is hard for you to kick against the goads.' —Acts 26:14

Why, why
do I kick against the goads?
What fear holds me back?
Don't I know
it takes a season
of dirtied hands tending
for a garden to grow?

Step into my fears
God will hold my hand
Pull the plank from my eye
Soon I will crawl
Soon I will stand.

Do not eat from the dung heap
Find the right soil
in which to plant.
Cultivate it, water it
Learning is earning
God only lights one step
in my path.

There is no harvest
without starting
No action
free from risk

Bow my knee
Bow my heart
Do what I can
in the Master's plan.

42. More Atheist T-Shirts

I have come that I may have life, and have it abundantly for ME. —Atheist John 10:10

Trust in ME with all MY heart; lean on MY own understanding. —Atheist Proverbs 3:5

In all MY ways acknowledge MYSELF, and I will make MY paths straight. —Atheist Proverbs 3:6

Go and make disciples of all nations, baptizing them in the name of ME. —Atheist Matthew 28:19

And we know that I work all things together for the good of ME, which is MY only purpose. —Atheist Romans 8:28

Finally, brothers, whatever is true, whatever is honorable, whatever is right, whatever is pure, whatever is lovely, whatever is admirable — if anything is excellent or praiseworthy — think these of ME. —Atheist Philippians 4:8

43. Eyes On

Let us fix our eyes on Jesus, the author and perfecter of our faith, who for the joy set before Him endured the cross, scorning its shame, and sat down at the right hand of the throne of God. —Hebrews 12:2

Are you looking to Jesus Christ?
"Bang! Ding! Crash!"
Did you look away?
"Watch this! Oh no! Sick!"
Eyes still on Jesus?
"Idiot! Did you see . . . I wonder . . . Gasp!"
How about now?

The Liar wins by
taking your eyes off Jesus Christ.
So don't let him.

Did you look away?
Look back to Jesus.
Own it
Apologize
Make right
Stay right

Keep your eyes upon Jesus,
Look full in His wonderful face,
And the things of earth will grow strangely dim,
In the light of His glory and grace.[8]

---

[8] Last paragraph is the chorus from "Turn Your Eyes upon Jesus" by Helen Howarth Lemmel (1922).

44. Slowly

Slowly slowly I creep
into decisions
I don't want to keep

Why why do I test
the Word's guidance
that leads to God's best?

Now now can I choose
to lean on Him
and make no excuse.

45. Come to Christ

Come
Come
How ever you are
It's not your behavior
It's simply your heart[9]

Come
Come
Day after day
A new way of living
Comes only this way

Come
Come
Into Christ's arms
Take refuge from trouble
His love weathers harm

Go
Go
In hand and hand
As ever He loves you
Spread His peace in this land.

---

[9] It is Jesus Christ that converts behavior! Not the other way round!

Come to Christ

Emmanuel Deweg

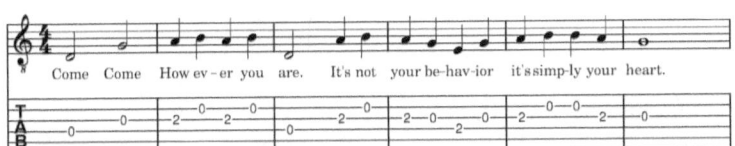
Come Come How ev-er you are. It's not your be-hav-ior it's simp-ly your heart.

Come Come Day af-ter day. A new way of liv-ing comes on-ly this way.

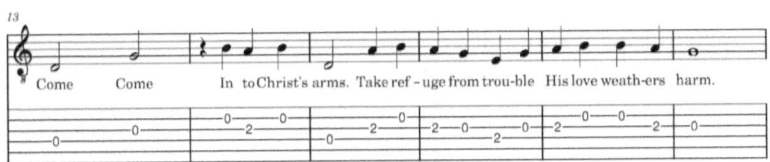
Come Come In to Christ's arms. Take ref-uge from trou-ble His love weath-ers harm.

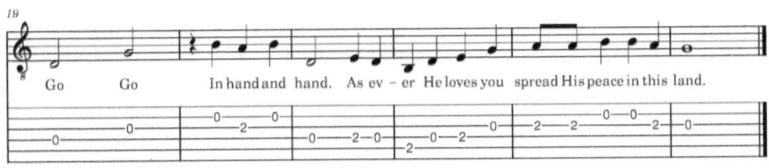
Go Go In hand and hand. As ev-er He loves you spread His peace in this land.

46. Desire

Archibald McCracket
collected everything
just to stack it.

Mariachi cassettes
stacked high by the door,
Bigotti plates,[10] magazines, figurines,
in neat piles across the floor.

What started out as fun
had gotten out of hand.
His desires overrode those of others;
Sadly, they can.

God gave us pleasures,
Rejoice that this is true,
when done through love
is what makes them good for you.

---

[10] Mr. McCracket is a big fan of "Larry-Boy and the Fib from Outer Space!"

47. *Katrina's Sun-Dial[11]

Hours fly,
    Flowers die:
New days,
New ways:
Pass by!
Love stays.

Time is
Too Slow for those who Wait,
Too Swift for those who Fear,
Too Long for those who Grieve,
Too Short for those who Rejoice;
  But for those who Love,
    Time is not.

---

[11] By Henry van Dyke Jr., European ambassador, Minister, and author of the book *The Other Wise Man* and song *Joyful, Joyful We Adore Thee*.

48. Ode to Ducks

In this, love has been perfected with us, so that we may have confidence in the day of judgment that, just as He is, also are we in this world. —1 John 4:17

They called her an ugly duck . . .

Born to a mother who was
a little over fourteen
in a town not impressive
its purpose unseen

The world dismissed her
with a sniff and a glance
This special child
was given no chance

And why should it?
How could it?

Growing up in a trailer
cussing like a sailor
Stealing gum
just for some fun

Her shoes too tight
Her pants too big
Her big rimmed glasses
all got teased in classes

The world judges by externals
attaching labels with staples and glue
But God sees internals
the heart inside that's true:

She fought for right
against every bully in sight
and ran with a thirst
to place always first

Some may have counted her out
but that's not what God's about
God knew this child would be
as magnificent as she

Now mother of three
and wife to me
Her home decorated with passion
in elegant French fashion

The hearts she helped mold
with God's love are untold
It's obvious today
what God knew right away

How ever you start
what matters is heart
though 'ducks' others may see
God makes us righteous as He![12]

---

[12] Another "duck" who God knew best was Louis Zamperini. Judge for yourself in his autobiography *Devil at My Heels*, or short book *Louis Zamperini: Redemption* by Janet & Geoff Benge.

49. Know

*You have turned things upside down, as if the potter
were regarded as clay. Shall what is formed say to him who formed it,
"He did not make me"? Can the pottery say of the potter,
"He has no understanding"? —Isaiah 29:16*

You don't
know
You don't know
How the Creator stretches out His hand
to spread light across this land

You don't
know
You don't know
How flowers were taught to grow
How rivers were taught to flow
Why the sparrow's heart sings
What today's love brings
What are the ways the wind comes
What are the ways that it goes

You don't
know
You don't know
Yet we speak all what's on our minds
before seeing that we were blind
We rail against every pain
but life without it is not the same
Saying how things ought to be
though where's the help from you and me?

When will the clay take a lesson and learn
our Father's will is for what we should yearn
Don't you
know
You don't know

50. It is Finished

If God exists, why doesn't He come down and show Himself?
He already did. Jesus came.[13]

If God exists, why doesn't He perform miracles?
He already does. Did you enjoy breathing today?

If God exists, why doesn't He make a way to stop evil?
He already did. Jesus through you.

If God exists, why doesn't He make us love Him?
He doesn't. That isn't love.

If God exists, why do people go to Hell?
Beats me. God has done everything so people can choose Heaven.

If God exists, why doesn't He create something so amazing, so unbelievable, so complex, and so unique that there can be no *doubt* He exists?
He already did. He created you.

---

[13] Plus the Old Testament! And His Holy Spirit is still here!

51. Vanity

When all has been heard, the conclusion of the matter is this: Fear God and keep His commandments, because this is the whole duty of man. —Ecclesiastes 12:13

How can I help you?
What do you need?
Make one more dollar?
Sell one more thneed?[14]

How about be the smartest?
Always a witty saying at hand?
Get a lot of "likes"?
Be famous across the land?

I know — power — authority — importance!
That's what you crave . . .
though there is no cure for the mirror
when you still feel like a knave.

So, what *are* we doing here?
What's it all about?
How can life be so empty
when stuff is *bursting* out?

After endless achievement
Solomon said the same
He checked every possibility
and was tops in all of life's games.

Want to know his conclusion
The answer is this —
Love God
Enjoy His gifts
The physical world is passing
Live in His Spirit to understand bliss.

---

[14] Theodor Geisel goes into great detail of this social problem in "The Lorax".

52. Lost

Immediately the boy's father cried out,
"I do believe; help my unbelief!" —Mark 9:24

I say I trust Jesus
but do I?
I say I'd give my life for Jesus
but would I?
I say Jesus means everything
but does He?
What am I missing?
What can't I see?
If there's power in the blood
what can't I feel it in me?

Why am I lazy
Why do I feel pain
Why am I greedy
Why am I mad when it rains

Am I holding on too tight
of my own control?
Is the problem my submission?
Mind, heart, body, and soul?

I feel like a lost sheep
Seeking direction
Seeking relief
Lord, help me in my unbelief!

53. Speed

Speed relates
time and distance
so drivers need <u>time</u>
to stop "this instant."

No matter the speed
what you need
count to 3
between "them and me"
as you race
gives the space
to stay alive
when you drive.

I lost all but one tooth
learning this trooth!

54. Age

But you have saved the fine wine until now! —John 2:10

As we get older
year after year
some age like wine
and some age like beer.
Which are you Dear?

55. God's Majority

For it is God's will that by doing good you should silence the ignorance of foolish men. —1 Peter 2:15

There's a faction
taking action
to convince God's Majority
that we have no Authority
over what we drink,
or what we wear,
or what we watch,
about what <u>we</u> care.

The faction loves to gloat
as they shove it down our throat
no matter how crude
they'll even be rude
pretending this dude
is a lady with 'tude.

Surprise surprise
we're actually alive!
This silenced Majority
has God's Authority
to vote with our feet
quietly, discreet,
not assenting to cloaked wrongs,
chanting songs,
or parading along.

We hold these truths
to be self-evident.[15]
Our Creator endowed us
with rights that are relevant

---

[15] Declaration of Independence

among these are life, liberty
and the pursuit of happiness
any faction's contractions
gets our scrappiness.

O-oh say, "It's Christ we obey"
He's the way every soul we can save
O'er the Land of the Freeeeee
and the Home of the Brave.

56. Change

The Copper Lady stands
lamp in hand
welcoming all to freedom's shores
> not to ease
> nor guarantees
She promises opportunity, nothing more.

"Give me your tired, your poor,
Your huddled masses yearning to breathe free,
The wretched refuse of your teeming shore.
Send these, the homeless, tempest-tossed to me,
I lift my lamp beside the golden door!"[16]

These peoples don't appear to be first rate
why alone, is America truly great?
Though other Nations failed
must we share their fate?

America happened for a reason
All we need is extend the season
The keys are few
Simply these two:

---

[16] Part of "The New Colossus" by Emma Lazarus November 2, 1883, which was written to raise funds for the Statue of Liberty, and was inscribed at the statue's base in 1903.

Continue the *Protection of Opportunity*
(possibilities stay open to those working in the community)[17]
And the *Protection of Success*
(no one will steal, tax, or penalize your earning's excess).[18]

These are why America stands dear
to every achiever far and near.

What then are *you* waiting for?
Opportunities abound, glimmering in view.
With whom does success start with?
Change starts with you!

---

[17] This is not equality of *results*, but open doors to the *opportunity* of success like education, home ownership, and business creation.

[18] The less reward, the less people strive, or they hide success (cash-based markets), or they leave to places of Protection ('voting with their feet'). Violations of Protections can be dollar based (overt taxation of income and spending, quiet taxes such as 'fees' or 'disability insurance', or hidden taxes such as inflation) or rule of law based (allowance of physical and material harm, or government intrusion and regulations). To analyze this in action, compare 2000 to 2020 populations shifts of Texas (+9M gains) and California (-1M loss) and ask, "Why?" See also *Why Nations Fail* by Nobel Economics Prize winners Daron Acemoglu and James A. Robinson or *The Other Path* by Hernando De Soto.

57. See All

By their fruit you will recognize them. Are grapes gathered from thornbushes, or figs from thistles? —Matthew 7:16

Please Professor Seezall
he tells me that he's honest
his words are really nice
how do I see what truth is?
To trust him or think twice?

"Zhe anzwer iz zo zimple
to zee vhat vords are true,
turn off hiz zound,
look all around,
and zee vhat he actually do!

"People vill zay anything
only trying to convince
but vhat about their actionz?
Actionz are heart'z evidence!"

Thank you Professor Seezall,
you have done it once again
this little test helps me see
to stay or run from my 'friend'.

A person's true heart
is easily found
all I must do is
"Turn off the Sound"!

58. Captain

Oh Captain
Which Captain
is navigating my ship?[19]
Setting speed, direction, destination,
and purpose for this trip

Is it the World
that buffets me in?
Every passing fad
twists me in the wind

Is it Me? Me. Me!
proudly standing at the wheel
with *no* idea where the ocean goes
self-doubt encrusted across my keel

Am I unequally yoked to another?
always fighting over the rudder . . .
I shudder.

Oh Captain
Which Captain
could navigate this ship?

'Tis the one that made the oceans
'Tis the one that made the lands
Invite Him to take over
And then you'll understand.

---

[19] Inspired from C. S. Lewis, *Mere Christianity*, Book Three, Chapter 1. (This footnote fulfills the requirement that all Christian books reference C. S. Lewis.)

59. Today

I planted the seed and Apollos watered it, but God made it grow.
—1 Corinthians 3:6

I may dream about tomorrow
of sights across the seas
but this is where God put me
so here I'm supposed to be

In *these* fields I shall toil
the harvest come what may
up to Him are all tomorrows
I'm to plant His love today.

60. Long Nose

The words of a gossip are like choice morsels that go down into the inmost being. —Proverbs 18:8

Who's that sneaking all around[20]
spreading gossip through the town
sliding tasty morsels down
It's Long Nose!

Who's that trying to get the digz
instead of minding their own biz
don't be caught by what they sez
It's Long Nose!

The morsels spread to you today
yours they'll spread another day
be careful what you say
To Long Nose!

---

[20] Have fun drawing your own sneaking Long Nose with "uuu" (left fingers), "U" (nose), "uuu" (right fingers), then the wall line, and finally the eyes and hair.

61. Sing

In the same way, I tell you that there will be more joy in heaven over one sinner who repents than over ninety-nine righteous ones who do not need to repent. —Luke 15:7

Who are you Man?
'How he came to believe?'
It doesn't matter!

It's all God's blessing
His theology is this:
Jesus Christ

"All I know is Jesus loves me and I love Jesus; I'm thankful, I know I'm not good enough, grateful that He *even Loves me*."

Hallelujah!
Let the Saints
Wherever sing!

62. Healed

*So I say, walk by the Spirit, and you will not gratify
the desires of the flesh. —Galatians 5:16*

How does one heal a physical addiction?
know that it isn't a spiritual affliction!

It comes down to who's in charge: heart or brain?
separate these to understand the two kinds of 'pain'.

Pain is not the same; Brain gets overloaded from things that taste death
but heart is eternal, created and beating and guided by God's breath.

The Spirit, God's breath, joined to our heart
is Lord of the flesh and all of its parts.

God knows the prescription for addiction that is simply the best:
Walk in His Spirit and break free from the rest.[21]

---

[21] Inspired by Alice Cooper's testimony, "God healed my alcoholism."

63. Planks

In the same way, on the outside you appear to be righteous, but on the inside you are full of hypocrisy and wickedness. —Matthew 23:28

I'm building me up a castle
from planks in my own eye
I stare, proud of its amazing grandeur
but God says it's a big ol' stinky sty.

I enjoy the feeling of importance
pointing out people's specks
though I should be giving grace to others
as God has forgiven me my debts.

Now when I point a finger
notice my other three
Who needs most improving?
They're all pointing back at me!

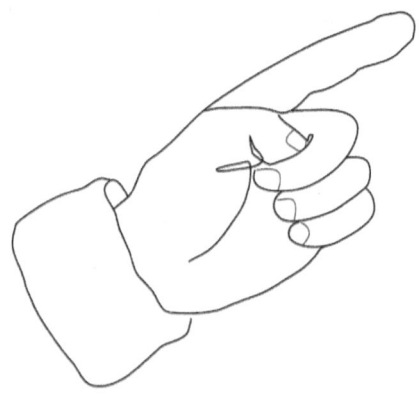

64. Moving Day!

Moving day!
All grown up and on your way
A new place, your own to stay
Decisions all will be your say
It's tough to let go of our girl that played
Your success in Christ we'll still pray
Moving day!

65. Relating Where

*For whoever does the will of God is
My brother and sister and mother. —Mark 3:35*

Who is my mother?
There are three that make the claim
but none that stay in the game
That's what I feel
on earth, none that are real.

The sign said, "family is forever"
(if you swallow their swill)
Earthly families are often outgrown
by growing in Christ's will.

Christ's family is for eternity
We're adopted, with rights same as He
His love joins us to one another
to live as sisters and brothers.

Back to the other, who is my mother?
None on earth but thrice as nice
God made all these wonderful women
my sisters *in Christ*.

Now I can let go of expectation
relating without obligation
such love is then free
just as God does for me.

66. Heart

Let no one deceive you with empty words . . . —Ephesians 5:6

how u been?

♥

glad u r good

♥

been rough here
burnt the food

♥

crashed my car

♥

then my dog
died

♥

glad i can count
on u. u being
there 4 me

♥

u r there right?

♥

this a joke?
heart everything?

♥

u r supposed 2 b
my friend

♥

no relationship
some stupid heart?

♥

i won't bother
u no more

♥

67. Little Birdie

Hey little birdie, we need you to
try real hard
Standing on our shoulders can only get
you so far

We know this means times where you're
sure to crash
Even though it hurts your hurts will
come to pass

It's hard for us to stand aside and let you
have such strife
'Tis the only way to grow strong enough to
own your life

Hey little birdie, just keep going you'll get stronger
after every try
You'll always be within our love so
time to fly

68. Bobblehead

a Bobblehead Boyfriend?
nodding 'yes' to everything you say
        your ego he feeds
            but 'flesh' are not needs
Partners of reeds can't stand in windy days

a Bobblehead Girlfriend?
affirming your every whim
          pumping up pride
          morals let slide
Who are you serving if you're not serving Him?

Fathers, brothers, buddies, sons
are you *man* enough to do
         what needs to be done?

Mothers, sisters, gal-pals, daughters
are you *woman* enough to do
         what you aught to?

Whatever our relation
we've *roles* in Creation
our responsibilities this hour:
           to lean on Christ
           listen to Christ
           and walk in Christ
His power empowers!
Hallelujah!

69. Brains in Chains

Don't buy the lie
free your brains from the chains
What you've been told won't hold
eternity is the name of the game

Their ad is a fad
pushing guilt to the hilt
with distraction from right action

But wealth is outside of self
in the Who that is True
immune to their tune
stand strong against wrong
sing the song of Him you belong.

70. Drink of God

Do you not know that your body is a temple of the Holy Spirit who is in you, whom you have received from God? You are not your own.
—1 Corinthians 6:19

Give up Church-y-anity
A-ban-done Religiosity
Through you, let the Holy Spirit see
That's how, to live in Jesus's love.

No more, do-do-doing
Let go, start be-be-being
Allow Christ, to verily be your King
To learn why the Good News sets you free.

Find in Him, your I-dentity
Which means, numbers count as empty
Love! is, the command from He
Who says the heart of mercy is most of all.

God's plan, includes even thee
Be joined, to the Trinity
Listen, yield, and move with agility
Spread His light where ever that you are.

Give up Church-y-anity
A-ban-done Religiosity
Tune in, for who you God too be[22]
That's how, to live in Jesus's love.

---

[22] To be clear, you are not God. God is the light and living water that flows through you to others to provide His righteousness and peace to us and this world. In this book where there can be interpretation of intent, know this: "Let God's truth reign supreme!"

71. Anxious

Be anxious about nothing, but in everything, by prayer and supplication with thanksgiving, let your requests be made known to God. —Philippians 4:6

Be anxious for nothing?
I'm anxious for something!

Every day on TV,
thieving and greed

Sitting in bed,
my phone fills me with dread

Did you see what she said?!
... I can't get it out of my head

And all my food in sight
the news reports it'll kill me tonight —

How do I end all of this worry?
What? Unplug my electronics?
But I'd be bored in a hurry![23]

---

[23] The note from Ross Ward at the Tinkertown Museum amongst the *thousands* of things he carved and created said, "I did this while you were watching TV."

72. Revolution

Do you think that I came to give peace on the earth? No, I say to you, but rather division. —Luke 12:51

Let's start a revolution
getting off that slippery slope
of hazy grays and truth buffets
trying to live by other people's dope

Demand the truth Demand the real
and Poke it with a Big Sharp stick
Test it all, debate and brawl
These ideas better be as solid as a brick

Build on Rock Build a house Build a life
Get Clarity not convolution
God's still here He's still right
— Find Him —
Let's start a revolution

73. Refuse the Ruse

Strings attached to things
Clouds
Heart from the start

The endower loves power
Why
A slave they crave

The getter no better
How
Greed makes the deed

Refuse the ruse

Tear the snare
Hear here
Obey His way

Get wealth, His self
Check
You live to give

The nose knows the rose.

74. Orange

Some people want all their poems to rhyme
Causing poets to insert random words like lemon or lime
        and with such imagination
           they avoid the reader's consternation
As long as the sentence doesn't end with "orange"

75. Relationship Recession

*He has raised up a horn of salvation for us
in the house of His servant David —Luke 1:69*

We're more informed than ever
about sports or the weather,
through when's the last time you did spy
people smiling and looking at each other in the eye?

Voices across the land echo confessions of depression
Why? a cultural Relationship Recession
commitments out of fashion,
our actions empty of compassion.

Wake up! Slumber no more!
Clean house! Kick those substitutes out the door!

You are part of God's cornucopia of empathy,
His empathy that spills over the hills and to the sea—
Break free of those fearful druthers
Be bold, fulfill your purpose, reach out and love others.

76. Ode to Lard

Let us feast and celebrate. —Luke 15:23

God's gift of food
Man takes apart
then puts it back together
charging more for this "art"!

Boneless, skinless
reconstituted nugget,
bottles and boxes filled
with who knows where they got it.

Man's food has more calories
and less nutrition,
so how sick must we get
before "convenience" becomes an imposition?

God's food prepared in His way
means experiencing the Real deal,
you'll also feel better
and take *pleasure* in the meal:

noshing on drumsticks,
nibbling apple cores,
gobbling pozole,
yogurt, kimchi, and more!

Bring on the schmaltz,
suet, and lard,
eating God's food
is easy, not hard.

77. Right Question

To whom gets wisdom and knowledge?
'tis not serendipity
        it starts at the question
        the *right* question
the question is the key

Wrong questions lure into the spurious
        losing time
        and dime
Right questions embolden the curious
        loosing brains
        for gains

What do answers alone address?
        not wisdom
        not knowledge
they're information, littered everywhere
answers alone just make a mess

Solve a question and see
        it's a riddle
        a puzzle
to get wisdom and knowledge
the right question is the key.[24]

---

[24] See also the "Five Whys" process in root cause analysis.

78. Mammon

You are not able to serve God and mammon. —Matthew 6:24

The struggles of man
are <u>part</u> of the plan.

Earning wealth for self —
what changes inside
when we realize
they're all left on the shelf?

For some they never change
even as the pulse leaves their vein
it moves not their core
to reach for God's golden door

Do we fritter away? we do
getting wants beyond food.
We must learn,
not just earn

What ever is gained
a pile,
low or high,
a pile the same

What is the point?
struggle but know
a body decays
while your spirit can grow.

79. Psalm 150

Let everything that has breath praise the LORD! —Psalm 150:6

Hallelu YAH[25]
Hallelu YAH
Let any thing that breathes
Praise the Lord!

boom rattle crash strum ting
rittle-tittle toot crash woosh ding
Let every thing with sound
Praise the Lord!

Let the Sun and the Stars
and the heavens and the Earth
Any thing that exists
say *through* its existence
Praise the Lord!
Praise the Lord!
Praise the Lord!

---

[25] We see this most often as Hallelujah, which is a combination of the Hebrew word to praise or boast ("halal" H1984 הָלַל) and Lord ("Yah" H3050 יָהּ).

80. Acceptance

Thanks be to God for His indescribable gift! —2 Corinthians 9:15

What does God say about you?
> He says I'm perfectly loved by Him.[26]

From when?
> Forever.[27]

How long does it last?
> Forever.[28]

And when you accepted Jesus, what did that make *you*?
> Complete.[29]

How much does He know about you?
> Everything.[30]

Everything?
> Everything.

Knowing everything, how did God *choose* to make *you*?
> Special.[31]

Being special and complete forever, when is God with you?
> Always.[32]

What then is holding you back from God's love?
> Acceptance.

---

[26] Psalm 18:30 "As for God, His way is perfect; the word of the LORD is flawless. He is a shield to all who take refuge in Him."

[27] Ephesians 1:4 "For He chose us in Him before the foundation of the world to be holy and blameless in His presence. In love . . ."

[28] 1 Chronicles 16:34 "Give thanks to the LORD, for He is good; His loving devotion endures forever."

[29] Hebrews 10:14 "For by one offering, He has [completed, finished, perfected, (teleioó, 5048)] for all time those being made holy."

[30] Psalm 139:1 "O LORD, You have searched me and known me."

[31] Psalm 139:14 "I praise You, for I am fearfully and [distinct, separated, set apart, wonderful (palah H6395)] made. Marvelous are Your works, and I know this very well."

[32] Deuteronomy 31:8 "The LORD Himself goes before you; He will be with you. He will never leave you nor forsake you. Do not be afraid or discouraged."

81. Minutes

*So teach us to number our days, that we may present
a heart of wisdom. —Psalm 90:12*

You may not have been born with a golden key
or beauty
or sports ability
There is one thing given to us all equally—
minutes
What are left of yours?

All day those clock hands are rollin'
some spend moanin'
others strollin'
when your skills and passions you could be honin'—
minutes
What do you do with yours?

See this, success is much your own creation
hard work has no limitation
proof is scattered across the nation
Now is *your* time to journey the paths of transformation—
minutes
What will you do with yours?

82. Aim For No Regrets

Godly sorrow brings repentance that leads to salvation without regret, but worldly sorrow brings death. —2 Corinthians 7:10

Shoulda Woulda Coulda
What's done is done
Own it, apologize, make right,
and live in love to prevent the next one

Today is yesterday's "one day"
Tomorrow's "one day" begins today
You may have mixed feelings about that
good or bad, life never stops where you're at

Do you lean on Him
when making life's grand plans?
Your greatest achievement could simply mean
being there, caring enough, to hold somebody's hand

Becoming the you that is new
from the who that you knew
comes from moving to the rhythm
of Christ in you.

Coulda Shoulda Woulda
for a life of no regrets
open your eyes and pray:
"Lord, let me see and sway
to whatever You say!"

83. Your Turn

84. Fight!

Ding Ding Ding
We're here live! at the ring
finishing up last night's fight
to determine the winer:
Who . . . is . . . most . . . right?

In this corner, the Wife
accused of being "in a mood"
(see how *he's* rude!)
that's what happens
dealing with his 'tude!

In this corner, the Husband
said he won't budge
you be the judge
being called "wimpy mouse"?
Who's the head of this house!?

There's the bell, so begins this bout
This promises to be one serious,
spousal, knock-down drag-out

They both leave their corners with haste . . .
rushing in to duke out the debate . . .
But wait!
        He's apologizing—
        She's apologizing—
        They're hugging—
        They're crying—
        Arm in arm,
        they are *leaving the ring!*

Ding Ding Ding
The Winner Is . . .
        LOVE!

85. Begin The End Begin

Soon you will pass away from here . . .
The one in the womb protests:
"But I am loved, happy, and cared for
and don't want to leave my comforts so dear."

The inevitable comes,
out of darkness and into light . . .
The baby looks up into a face of love
cradled and protected, awed by their new home
"What a wonderful place, if only I'd known . . ."

The years pass
Baby to youth to maturity
A marriage. A family.
Excitement and strife,
struggles, laughter, rewards of life.

Soon you will pass away from here . . .
The elder protests:
"But I am loved, happy, and cared for
and don't want to leave my comforts so dear."

The inevitable comes,
out of darkness and into light . . .
The new-born looks up into The Face of Love
cradled and protected, awed by their new home
"What a wonderful place, if only I'd known . . ."

About the Author

Emmanuel DeWeg is a Dutch pseudonym which means "God with us" "is the Way". Emmanuel ("God with us") is the name given to Jesus in Matthew 1:23 to fulfill the prophesy in Isaiah 7:14. DeWeg ("the Way") is God's plan for salvation through Jesus Christ (prophesied by Isaiah 30:21, proclaimed by Jesus in John 14:6, and used by the first Church in Acts 9:2).

The "author" is a disciple of Jesus Christ, without special title, trying to live best in this world through Him. He looks to God, His written word (the Bible), and God's disciples (the body of Christ) here on earth for guidance, as should any study group to settle all discussion. In other words, the answer to any debate should be, "What does God say about that and how do we apply it from *His love*?"

Like those cited by Jesus of "great faith" (Matthew 8:10 and Matthew 15:28) our goal is to be as His children, yield our hearts to God, and let *His righteousness* flow through unique us. There is no magic formula or specific action, since the Trinity + You is *unique*. Everything flows from that relationship.

God loves you. Now go and live like it.

For comments or contributions to this edition, free resources, or to subscribe to future release information, please go to the publisher's website: EmmanuelDeWeg.org

www.ingramcontent.com/pod-product-compliance
Lightning Source LLC
Chambersburg PA
CBHW021627080526
44585CB00013BA/904